Dagmar Geisler

Short Witch Stories

Translated by Sabrina Erfurth

arsEdition

Bibliografische Information Der Deutschen Bibliothek

Die Deutsche Bibliothek verzeichnet diese Publikation
in der Deutschen Nationalbibliografie;
detaillierte bibliografische Daten sind im Internet über
http://dnb.ddb.de abrufbar.

5 4 3 2 1 08 07 06 05

Originaltext, Titelbild, Innenillustrationen: Dagmar Geisler
Übersetzung ins Englische: Sabrina Erfurth
Titelvignette: Carola Holland
ISBN 3-7607-4026-X

Kleine Hexengeschichten

Text, Titelbild, Innenillustrationen: Dagmar Geisler

Konzeption und Umsetzung des Lernspielheftes: Sabrina Erfurth
Die CD wurde aufgenommen in Berlin, Januar 2005
Sprecherin: Rebecca Stodiek
Aufnahme: Jasper Diederich
Musik, Regie, Gesamtproduktion: Thomas Lotz

www.arsedition.de

Contents

Where is the Witch Hat?

Flora the witch is angry.
Her witch hat is gone.
Yesterday her hat was still there.
Today it's gone.

Flora looks
under her bed
and behind the door.
She looks in the pantry
and in the bathroom.
She can't find her hat anywhere.

She asks Max the raven:
"Did you hide my hat?"
"Why me?" Max croaks.
"What would I want your hat for?"

"I don't know either,"
grumbles Flora.
"At least help me look for it, then."

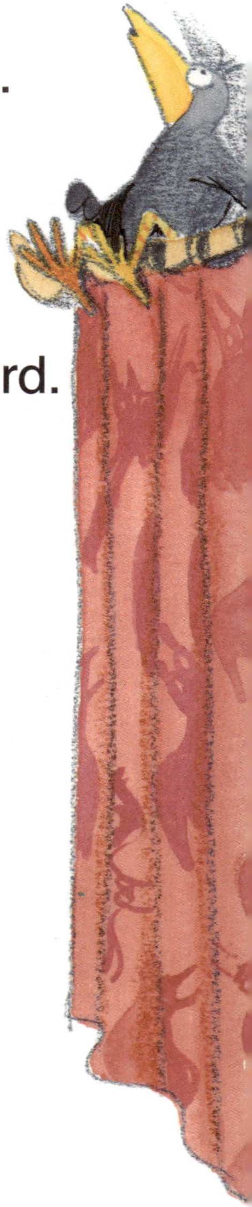

Flora searches in the kitchen.
Max searches
on the curtain rod.
Flora searches on the shelf.
Max searches on the cupboard.

"What a nuisance,"
complains Flora.
"I can't go out
without my hat."

"Take a head scarf," says Max.
"Maybe the one
with the snail pattern.
Or the garish green one
with the earthworms."

Flora is annoyed.
She can't stand head scarves.
"I'll never wrap
a head scarf
around my head."

"You can't be a witch without
something on your head," says Max.
"I want my hat!" shouts Flora.

She runs outside.
And stops puzzled.
She can't believe her eyes.

"Hello, Flora!" calls Susi the raven.
"Would you like to have a look at
our children?
They hatched last night."

“Last night there was a storm.
It tore the whole nest to pieces.
And that is why we had to borrow
your hat for a short while,”
Max says shamefaced.

“Oh!” Flora grins.
”Then I will have to wear
a head scarf for a while.
Maybe the one with the cheeky
raven pattern.”

The Witch Exam

Flora the witch likes to dawdle.
She would like to be punctual,
but something
always distracts her.

Today there's a witch exam.
She has to be there on time.

Max the raven says goodbye
at the door.
He says: "Don't dawdle again.
Remember the Supreme Witch."
"Yes, I know,"
says Flora
and grabs her magic wand.

She has to pass
the witch exam.
Then she'll finally get
her broomstick.
That will be great.

Then she sees something
lying next to the path.
Shoes with wheels,
how interesting.

Of course, she has to
try them out quickly.
The shoes even fit.

The first steps
are a little shaky.
But then the shoes speed up.
Cool!

But maybe
a little too fast.
"Stop!" Flora screams.

She whizzes towards the city
incredibly fast.
How on earth
can you stop these things?
"Out of the way!" Flora bellows.
People jump aside.

The house can’t jump away.
Flora conjures
a nice arch
and zooms through it.

The tram stops
in the middle of the crossing.
Abracadabra!
And just like that,
it floats as a zeppelin
above the city.

Oh no, the weekly market!
Today of all days!

Flora rams the lady selling flowers.
She brushes the man
with the balloons.
She rolls over the fresh eggs.

There is
butcher Meier's stall.
Faster and faster
Flora races towards it.
What can she do?

At the last moment
she sends the whole market
on top of the town hall roof.
The square is nice and empty now.

Relieved, Flora turns around
once more,
stumbles and goes flying
into the river.

Splash!
Suddenly she remembers
the witch exam.
Now she will be too late.
What will the Supreme Witch say?

Anxiously,
Flora sets off.
Up on the mountain
they are already waiting for her.
“You are not on time again,”
says the Supreme Witch strictly.

“But you have passed
the witch exam.
We saw
everything.
You did very well!”

Flora gets a brand new
broomstick.
Then she celebrates wildly
with the others
until late in the night.

The Witch Bath

"It's about time again,"
says Max, the raven.
"Hm," Flora groans.
She is reading
the witch's newspaper
and isn't listening at all.

“It’s about time again,”
Max says a little louder.
“What are you talking about?”
Flora asks.
Max explains that it is time
for a bath.

”Oh no!” Flora cries.
“Oh yes!” says Max.

Flora doesn’t like baths.
She finds herself witch-clean.

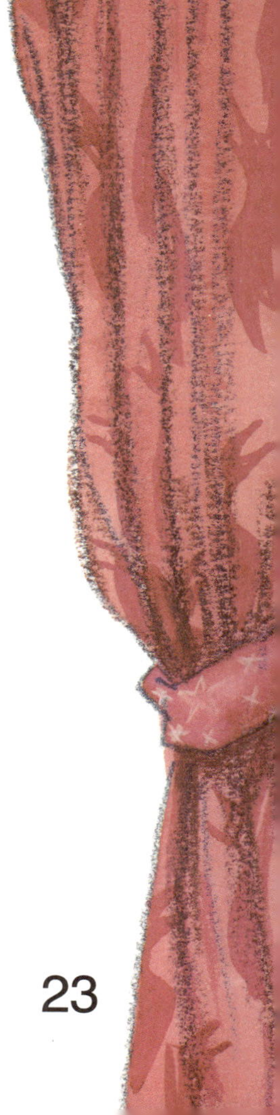

Her toes are nice and black.
Her fingernails have
great, green witch marks.
Her knees are as grey
as they should be.
And the dirt
in her ears
crackles nicely,
especially
when she is
falling asleep.

She grumbles:
"I took a bath
just ten years ago."
"Exactly twenty years
and three months ago," says Max.

Flora looks for more excuses.
The Goldfish family
lives in the bathtub.

Max has already
brought them to the pond.

Flora hasn't got any more
witch's bath foam.
Max knows where the recipe is.

Max helps to stir
until everything foams nicely.
He turns on the water.

Flora takes off her clothes.
"But no washing my hair,"
she snarls.

She sticks her fat toe
into the water.
“By the way, why don’t you
take a bath, Max?”

“I’m not a duck!”
croaks Max indignantly.
“Well, am I?”
Flora asks.

Finally she is lying
in the tub.
The water bubbles.
Max is totally exhausted.

“Wonderful!” Flora sighs.
“I could stay in here
until Easter.”

“It’s always the same!”
croaks Max.

The Birthday

Flora is sitting at
the kitchen table.
She is practicing witchcraft.
She wants to turn
old hats into witch
cakes.

This is difficult.
First the hats
turn into hard rolls
and then into spinach with fried eggs.
Ugh!

Max is sitting on the curtain rod
and is croaking
at the top of his voice.

“Can’t you sing quieter?”
asks Flora.
Max continues to croak.

Flora turns the hats
into wilting heads of lettuce.
“You’re getting on my nerves!”
she growls.
Max continues to croak.

"Now shut
your trap,
you noisy brat!"
screams Flora.
"Did you actually
say noisy brat?"
Max asks angrily.

"Exactly," shouts Flora.
"Horrible noisy brat!"

"You know nothing
about music!"
croaks Max.

Insulted, he flutters
up and away.

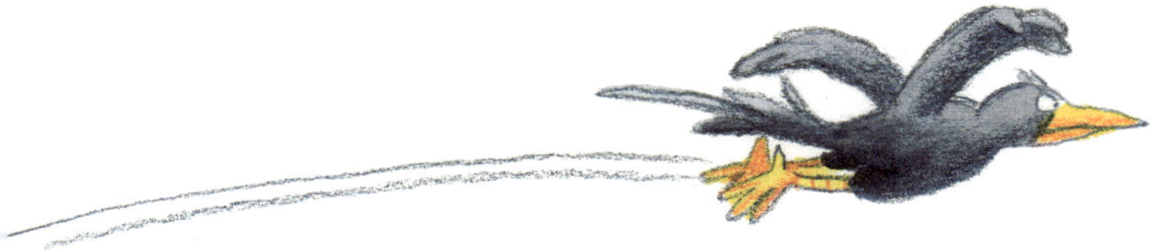

Now it is quiet
in the kitchen.
Flora wants to make witch cakes.
But she is thinking of Max.
The hats turn
into pumpkins.

Flora sighs.
Where could Max have flown to?

In the evening
Max still isn't back.
And the hats
are still hats.

"Tomorrow is my birthday,"
Flora thinks sadly.
"But without Max
and without a cake
I'd rather stay in bed."

Even in the morning
Max is nowhere to be seen.
Flora pulls the blanket
over her head.

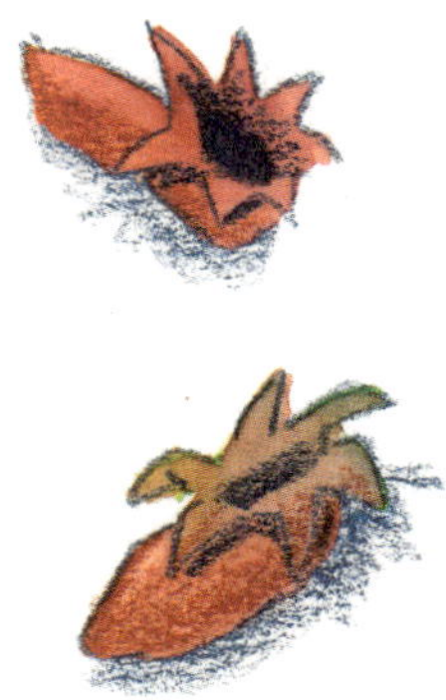

Then she hears voices
in the garden.
She shuffles to the door.

The other witches
are standing outside.
They are holding a big witch cake.

"Isn't it your birthday today?"
asks the Swamp Witch.

"Yes," says Flora.
"But have you seen Max?
He's been gone since yesterday."

But nobody has seen the raven.
And without Max
even the best cake
doesn't taste good.

Suddenly there's a croak
from up in the tree.
Max is sitting there
with a whole raven orchestra.

“Happy birthday to you”
he sings. And: “I kiss your hand, madam.”

“Dreadfully beautiful!”
groans the Root Witch.
Then Max sings an encore:
“A friend, a good friend …”

“Oh, Max!” Flora cheers.
“I will never call you
a noisy brat again.”
Max grins.

Vocabulary List

Vokabelliste

A a	ein(e); ▶ a little
a little	ein bisschen; etwas
about	über; von; ▶ it's about time
actually	eigentlich; etwa
again	wieder; ▶ never again
ago	vor
all	▶ isn't listening at all; ▶ today of all days
already	schon
always	immer
am	bin (to be = sein)
an	ein(e)
and	und
angry	sauer, wütend
angrily	sauer, wütend
annoyed	genervt
anxiously	ängstlich
any	▶ hasn't got … any more
anywhere	▶ can't find … anywhere
arch	der Torbogen
are	bist; sind (to be = sein)
around	um
as	als; ▶ as grey as
as grey as	so grau wie
aside	zur Seite
asks	fragt (to ask = fragen)

asleep	▶ falling asleep
at	▶ not at all; ▶ at least; ▶ at the top of his voice; ▶ have a look at
at least	wenigstens
at the top of his voice	aus vollem Halse
away	weg; ▶ up and away

B

back	▶ isn't back
balloons	die Luftballons
bath	baden; das Bad; ▶ bath foam
bath foam	der Badeschaum
bathroom	das Badezimmer; das Klo
baths	die Bäder
bathtub	die Badewanne
be	sein; ▶ be too late; ▶ nowhere to be seen
be too late	zu spät kommen
beautiful	schön
bed	das Bett
been	▶ He's been gone since yesterday.
behind	hinter
believe	glauben; ▶ can't believe her eyes
bellows	brüllt (to bellow = brüllen)
best	beste; bester
big	groß
birthday	der Geburtstag; ▶ Happy Birthday to you.
black	schwarz
blanket	die Decke
borrow	ausleihen
brand new	nagelneu
brat	▶ noisy brat
broomstick	der Hexenbesen
brought	gebracht; brachte
brushes	streift (to brush = streifen)
bubbles	blubbert (to bubble = blubbern); die Blasen; ▶ soap bubbles
but	aber; doch

butcher	der Metzger
by	bei; ▶ by the way
by the way	eigentlich; übrigens
C cake	der Kuchen (birthday cake = die Geburtstagstorte; der Geburtstagskuchen)
cakes	die Kuchen
call	rufen; ▶ call you
call you …	dich … nennen (call somebody something = jemanden etwas nennen)
calls	ruft (to call = rufen)
can	kann; können
can't	kann nicht (Kurzform von "cannot"); ▶ can't believe her eyes; ▶ can't find … anywhere; ▶ can't stand
can't believe her eyes	kann ihren Augen nicht trauen (to believe one's eyes = seinen Augen trauen)
can't find … anywhere	kann ... nirgends finden
can't stand	kann nicht ausstehen
celebrates	feiert (to celebrate = feiern)
cheeky	frech
cheers	jubelt (to cheer = jubeln)
children	die Kinder
city	die Stadt
clothes	▶ takes off her clothes
complains	schimpft (to complain = schimpfen)
conjures	hext (to conjure = hexen)
continues	macht weiter (to continue = weiter machen)
cool	schön; cool; toll
could	könnte
course	▶ of course
crackles	knistert (to crackle = knistern)
cries	schreit (to cry = schreien)
croak	krächzen; krähen

croaking	krächzt (to croak = krächzen)
croaks	krächzt; kräht (to croak = krächzen; krähen)
crossing	die Kreuzung
cup	der Becher
cupboard	der Schrank
curtain rod	die Gardinenstange
D	
dawdle	trödele; trödelt (to dawdle = trödeln)
days	die Tage; ▶ today of all days
did	gemacht (to do = machen); ▶ did you hide …; ▶ did you say
did you hide …	hast du … versteckt (to hide something = etwas verstecken)
did you say …	hast du … gesagt (to say something = etwas sagen)
difficult	schwierig
dirt	der Schmutz
distracts	lenkt ab (to distract somebody = jemanden ablenken)
do	tun (to do = tun); ▶ What can she do?
doesn't	▶ doesn't like; ▶ doesn't taste good (Kurzform von „does not" = tut nicht)
doesn't like	mag nicht
doesn't taste good	schmeckt nicht
don't	▶ I don't know.; ▶ Why don't you take a bath? (Kurzform von „do not" = nicht tun)
door	die Tür
dreadfully	schaurig
duck	die Ente; ▶ duck weed
duck weed	die Entengrütze
E	
ears	die Ohren
earth	die Erde; ▶ How on earth can you …?
earthworms	die Regenwürmer
Easter	Ostern
eggs	die Eier ▶ fried eggs

(not ...) either	auch nicht
empty	leer
encore	die Zugabe
especially	besonders
even	auch; sogar
evening	der Abend
everything	alles
exactly	genau
exam	die Prüfung
excuses	die Ausreden
exhausted	erschöpft
explains	erklärt (to explain = erklären)
eyes	die Augen; ▶ can't believe her eyes

F

falling asleep	einschlafen
family	die Familie
fast	schnell
faster and faster	immer schneller
fat	dick; dicke
finally	endlich
find	finden
finds	findet (to find = finden)
fingernails	die Fingernägel
first	zuerst; ▶ the first
fit	passen
floats	schwebt (to float = schweben)
flowers	die Blumen
flown	geflogen (to fly = fliegen)
flutters	flattert (to flutter = flattern)
flying	▶ goes flying into
foam	Schaum ▶ bath foam
foams	schäumt (to foam = schäumen)
for	auf; für
fresh	frisch
fried eggs	die Spiegeleier
friend	der Freund
from	von

G

garden	der Garten
garish green	giftgrün
get	bekommt (to get = bekommen; werden)
gets	bekommt (to get = bekommen)
getting	▶ You're getting on my nerves!
glass	das Glas
go	gehen
goes flying into	fliegt hinein (to go flying into something = in etwas hineinfliegen)
goldfish	der Goldfisch
gone	verschwunden; weg
good	gut
goodbye	Auf Wiedersehen ▶ says goodbye
got	▶ hasn't got … anymore
grabs	schnappt (to grab = schnappen)
great	toll
green	grün; ▶ garish green
grey	grau
grins	grinst (to grin = grinsen)
groans	brummt; grummelt (to groan = brummen; grummeln)
grounded	gemahlen
growls	knurrt (to growl = knurren)
grumbles	mault; brummt (to grumble = maulen; brummen

H

had to	musste (to have to = müssen)
hair	die Haare
hall	die Halle; ▶ town hall
hand	die Hand
Happy Birthday to you.	Herzlichen Glückwunsch zum Geburtstag.
hard	hart
has	hast; ▶ has to
has to	muss (to have to = müssen)
hasn't got … any more	hat kein … mehr (Kurzform von “has not got … anymore“)
hat	der Hut

hatched	geschlüpft (to hatch = schlüpfen)
hats	die Hüte
have	habt; hast (to have = haben); ▶ have a look at
have a look at	ansehen (to have a look at = ansehen)
he	er
head	der Kopf
head scarf	das Kopftuch
head scarves	die Kopftücher
heads	die Köpfe
hears	hört (to hear = hören)
hello	hallo
help	hilf (to help = helfen)
helps	hilft
her	ihre(n); sie; ihr
here	hier
herself	sich (weiblich: sie sich)
He's been gone since yesterday.	Er ist seit gestern weg.
hide	versteckt (to hide = verstecken)
his	sein
holding	halten (to hold = halten)
horrible	schrecklich
house	das Haus
how	wie
How on earth can you …?	Wie kannst du bloß …?

I

I	ich
I'd	ich würde (Kurzform von „I would“)
I don't know.	Ich weiß nicht.
I'll	ich werde (Kurzform von „I will“)
I'm	ich bin (Kurzform von „I am“)
in	in; ▶ in the middle of
in the middle of	mitten auf; inmitten
incredibly fast	rasend schnell
indignantly	empört
insulted	beleidigt

interesting	interessant
into	in
is	ist (to be = sein)
isn't	ist nicht (Kurzform von "is not")
isn't back	ist nicht zurück (to be back = zurück
sein)	
it	es
it's	es ist (Kurzform von „it is"); ▶ it's about time
it's about time	es ist soweit
J jump	springen
just	erst; ▶ just like that
just like that	plötzlich; schon
K kiss	küsse (to kiss = küssen); der Kuss
kitchen	die Küche
knees	die Knie
know	weiß, weißt; verstehst (to know = wissen; verstehen)
knows	weiß (to know = wissen; verstehen)
L lady	die Frau; die Dame
last	letzte(r)
late	spät
least	▶ at least
lettuce	der Salat
like	mag; ▶ just like that; ▶ like to
like to ...	gern ... machen (to like to do something = gerne etwas machen)
listening	hört zu (to listen = zuhören)
little	▶ a little
lives	wohnt (to live = leben; wohnen)
look at	ansehen
look for	suchen
looks for	sucht (to look for = suchen)
louder	lauter
lying	liegen; liegt (to lie = liegen)

M

madam	die Madam, das Fräulein
magic wand	der Zauberstab
make	machen
man	der Mann
market	der Markt; ▶ weekly market
marks	die Flecken
maybe	vielleicht
me	ich; mir
moment	der Moment
months	die Monate
more	mehr; ▶ once more
morning	der Morgen
mountain	der Berg
music	die Musik
my	mein(e)

N

nerves	Nerven; ▶ You're getting on my nerves!
nest	das Nest
never	niemals; ▶ never again
never again	nie mehr
new	neu; ▶ brand new
newspaper	die Zeitung
next to	neben
nice	schön
nicely	schön
night	der Abend; die Nacht
no	nein
nobody	niemand
noisy brat	der Schreihals
not at all	gar nicht
not on time	unpünktlich
nothing	nichts
now	jetzt
nowhere to be seen	nirgends zu sehen
nuisance	▶ what a nuisance

O	of	von; ▶ in the middle of; ▶ of course; ▶ on top of; ▶ thinking of; ▶ today of all days
	of course	natürlich
	off	▶ sets off; ▶ takes off her clothes
	old	alt
	on	auf; ▶ How on earth can you …?; ▶ on time; ▶ on top of; ▶ You're getting on my nerves!
	on time	pünktlich
	on top of	auf; oben auf
	once more	noch einmal
	one	eins; ▶ the one
	or	oder
	orchestra	das Orchester
	other	andere; ▶ the other; ▶ the others
	our	unsere
	out	aus; ▶ try them out
	outside	draußen
	over	über
P	pantry	die Speisekammer
	pass the exam	die Prüfung bestehen
	passed the exam	die Prüfung bestanden (to pass an exam = eine Prüfung bestehen)
	path	der Weg
	pattern	das Muster
	people	die Leute
	pieces	die Einzelteile; ▶ tore … to pieces
	pond	der Teich
	practicing witchcraft	hexen (to practice witchcraft = hexen)
	pulls	zieht (to pull = ziehen)
	pumpkins	die Kürbisse
	punctual	pünktlich
	puzzled	verdutzt
Q	quickly	schnell
	quiet	ruhig

	quieter	leiser
R	races	rast (to race = rasen)
	rams	rammt (to ram = rammen)
	rather	lieber
	raven	der Rabe
	reading	liest (to read = lesen)
	recipe	das Rezept
	relieved	erleichtert
	remember	denk an (to remember something = an etwas denken)
	remembers ...	fällt ... ein (to remember something = einem fällt etwas ein)
	river	der Fluss
	rod	die Stange; ▶ curtain rod
	rolls	rollt (to roll = rollen); die Semmeln
	roof	das Dach
	root	die Wurzel
	runs	rennt (to run = rennen)
S	sadly	traurig
	saliva	die Spucke
	same	dasselbe
	saw	gesehen, sah (to see = sehen)
	say	sagen
	says	sagt (to say = sagen); ▶ says goodbye
	says goodbye	verabschiedet sich (to say goodbye = sich verabschieden)
	scarf	der Schal; ▶ head scarf
	scarves	die Schals; ▶ head scarves
	screams	schreit (to scream = schreien)
	scrubbing sand	der Scheuersand
	searches	sucht (to search = suchen)
	seen	gesehen (to see = sehen); ▶ nowhere to be seen
	sees	sieht (to see = sehen)
	selling	verkauft (to sell = verkaufen)

sends	schickt (to send = schicken)
sets off	macht sich auf den Weg (to set off = sich auf den Weg machen)
shaky	wacklig
shamefaced	verschämt
she	sie
she'll	sie wird (Kurzform von „she will“)
she's	sie ist (Kurzform von “she is”)
shelf	das Regal
shoes	die Schuhe
short	kurz; klein; ▶ short while
short while	kurz(e Weile)
should	sollen
shouts	brüllt; schreit (to shout = brüllen; schreien)
shuffles	schlurft (to shuffle = schlurfen)
shut your trap	halt den Schnabel (to shut your trap = den Schnabel halten)
sighs	seufzt (to sigh = seufzen)
since	seit
sing	singen
sings	singt (to sing = singen)
sitting	sitzt (to sit = sitzen)
snail	die Schnecke
snarls	knurrt (to snarl = knurren)
soap	die Seife
soap bubbles	die Seifenblasen (Pustefix)
some	ein wenig; etwas
something	etwas; irgendetwas
speed up	in Fahrt geraten
spinach	der Spinat
Splash!	Platsch!
spoonful	ein Löffel voll
square	der Platz
stall	der Stand
stand	stehen; ▶ can't stand
standing	stehen (to stand = stehen)
stay	bleibe; bleiben

steps	die Schritte
sticks … into the water	… ins Wasser halten (to stick something into the water = etwas ins Wasser halten)
still	immer noch
stir	rühren
stop	halt (to stop = anhalten)
stops	bleibt stehen; hält (to stop = anhalten; stehenbleiben)
stories	die Geschichten
storm	das Unwetter; der Sturm
strictly	streng
stumbles	stolpert (to stumble = stolpern)
suddenly	auf einmal
supreme witch	die Oberhexe
swamp	das Moor
syrup	der Sirup

T

table	der Tisch
take	nimm (to take = nehmen); ▶ take a bath
take a bath	baden
takes off her clothes	zieht sich aus (to take off one's clothes = sich ausziehen)
talking	redest (to talk = reden)
taste	schmecken
ten	zehn
that	das; dass; ▶ that is why
that is why	darum
the	der; die; das
the first	die erste(n)
the one	das; der, die, das ein(e)
the other(s)	die anderen
them	sie (Plural)
then	da; dann
there	da
there's	da ist (Kurzform von "there is")
these	diese

they	sie (Plural)
things	die Dinge(r)
thinking	denken
thinking of	denkt an (to think of something = an etwas denken)
thinks	denkt (to think = denken)
this	das
three	drei
through	hindurch
time	die Zeit; ▶ it's about time; ▶ on time
to	zu; zur
toad	die Kröte
today	heute; ▶ today of all days
today of all days	ausgerechnet heute
toe	der Zeh
toes	die Zehen
tomorrow	morgen
too	zu
took a bath	badete; gebadet (to take a bath = baden)
top	oben; ▶ at the top of his voice; ▶ on top of
tore … to pieces	hat ... zerfetzt (to tear something to pieces = etwas zerfetzen)
totally	ganz
towards	drauf zu
town hall	das Rathaus
tram	die Straßenbahn
trap	die Falle; ▶ shut your trap
tree	der Baum
try out	die … ausprobieren (to try something out = etwas ausprobieren)
tub	die Wanne
turn … into	… in … verwandeln (to turn something into something = etwas in etwas verwandeln)

turns ... into ...	verwandelt ... in ... ; verhext (to turn into = verhexen); ▶ turns around; ▶ turns up
turns around	dreht sich um (to turn around = sich umdrehen)
turns up	dreht auf (to turn up = aufdrehen)
twenty	zwanzig

U

Ugh!	Brr!
under	unter
until	bis
up	oben; ▶ speed up; ▶ turns up; ▶ up and away
up and away	auf und davon

V

very	sehr
voice	die Stimme; ▶ at the top of his voice
voices	die Stimmen

W

waiting for	erwartet (to wait for = erwarten)
wand	▶ magic wand
want	will; wollen
wants	will
was	war (to be = sein)
washing	waschen
water	das Wasser
way	der Weg; ▶ by the way
we	wir
wear	tragen (auf Kleidung bezogen)
weed	▶ duck weed
weekly market	der Wochenmarkt
well	nun; toll
what	was; wovon; ▶ what a nuisance
what a nuisance	zu dumm
What can she do?	Was tun?
wheels	die Räder

where	wo
while	die Weile; beim; während; ▶ short while
whizzes	saust (to whizz = sausen)
whole	ganz
why	warum; wieso; ▶ that is why; ▶ Why don't you take a bath?
Why don't you take a bath?	Warum badest du nicht?
wildly	wild
will	werde (will = werden (Zukunft))
wilting	welk
witch	die Hexe; ▶ supreme witch
witch-clean	hexensauber
witchcraft	Hexerei; ▶ practicing witchcraft
witches	die Hexen
with	mit
without	ohne
wonderful	herrlich
woodruff	Waldmeister
would	würde (would = würden)
wrap	binde (to wrap = binden)

Y

years	die Jahre
yes	doch; ja; stimmt
yesterday	gestern
you	du
You're getting on my nerves!	Du nervst! (Kurzform von "you are ...")
your	dein(e)

Z

zeppelin	der Zeppelin
zooms	braust (to zoom = brausen)

Dagmar Geisler

Kleine Hexengeschichten

Wo ist der Hexenhut?

Hexe Flora ist sauer.
Ihr Hexenhut ist weg.
Gestern war der Hut noch da.
Heute ist er weg.

Flora sucht
unter dem Bett
und hinter der Tür.
Sie sucht in der Speisekammer
und auf dem Klo.
Nirgends ist der Hut zu finden.

Sie fragt Max, den Raben:
„Hast du meinen Hut versteckt?"
„Wieso ich?", krächzt Max.
„Was soll ich mit deinem Hut?"

„Weiß ich auch nicht",
brummt Flora.
„Dann hilf mir wenigstens suchen."

Flora sucht in der Küche.
Max sucht
auf der Gardinenstange.
Flora sucht im Regal.
Max sucht auf dem Schrank.

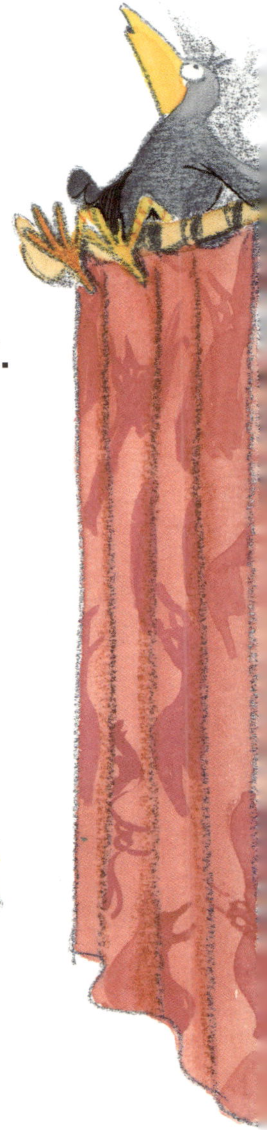

„Zu dumm", schimpft Flora.
„Ohne meinen Hut
kann ich nicht
aus dem Haus gehen."

„Nimm ein Kopftuch“, sagt Max.
„Vielleicht das
mit dem Schneckenmuster.
Oder das giftgrüne
mit den Regenwürmern.“

Flora ist genervt.
Kopftücher kann sie
nicht ausstehen.
„Niemals binde ich
ein Kopftuch um.“

„Ohne etwas auf dem Kopf
kannst du nicht hexen“, sagt Max.
„Ich will meinen Hut!“, schreit Flora.

Sie rennt nach draußen.
Und bleibt verdutzt stehen.
Sie traut ihren Augen nicht.

„Hallo, Flora!“, ruft Susi Rabe.
„Willst du dir
unsere Kinder ansehen?
Sie sind heute Nacht geschlüpft.“

„Gestern Abend war ein Unwetter.
Es hat das ganze Nest zerfetzt.
Und darum mussten wir kurz
deinen Hut ausleihen“,
sagt Max verschämt.

„Oh!“ Flora grinst.
„Dann muss ich eine Weile
doch ein Kopftuch tragen.
Vielleicht das
mit dem frechen Rabenmuster.“

Die Hexenprüfung

Hexe Flora trödelt gern.
Sie möchte pünktlich sein,
aber irgendetwas
lenkt sie immer ab.

Heute ist Hexenprüfung.
Da muss sie pünktlich sein.

Rabe Max verabschiedet sich
an der Tür.
Er sagt: „Trödle nicht wieder.
Denk an die Oberhexe.“
„Ja, ja“, sagt Flora
und schnappt sich
ihren Zauberstab.

Die Hexenprüfung
muss sie bestehen.
Dann bekommt sie endlich
ihren Hexenbesen.
Das wird toll.

Da sieht sie am Weg
etwas liegen.
Schuhe mit Rädern,
wie interessant.

Die muss sie natürlich
schnell ausprobieren.
Die Schuhe passen sogar.

Die ersten Schritte
sind etwas wacklig.
Doch dann kommen die Schuhe
in Fahrt. Schön!

Aber vielleicht
ein bisschen schnell.
„Halt!“, schreit Flora.

Sie saust rasend schnell
auf die Stadt zu.
Wie bremst man die Dinger bloß?
„Aus dem Weg!“, brüllt Flora.
Leute springen zur Seite.

Das Haus kann nicht wegspringen.
Flora hext ihm einen
schönen Torbogen
und braust hindurch.

Die Straßenbahn hält
mitten auf der Kreuzung.
Hexifexifax!
Schon schwebt sie
als Zeppelin
über der Stadt.

Oh nein, der Wochenmarkt.
Ausgerechnet heute!

Flora rammt die Blumenfrau.
Sie streift den Mann
mit den Luftballons.
Sie rollt über frische Landeier.

Da steht der Stand
von Metzger Meier.
Immer schneller rast
Flora darauf zu.
Was tun?

Im letzten Moment
hext sie den ganzen Markt
auf das Rathausdach.
Schön leer ist der Platz jetzt.

Erleichtert dreht Flora
sich noch einmal um,
stolpert und fliegt
in hohem Bogen
in den Fluss.

Platsch!
Da fällt ihr die Hexenprüfung
wieder ein.
Jetzt kommt sie zu spät.
Was wird die Oberhexe sagen?

Ängstlich macht sich
Flora auf den Weg.
Oben am Berg wird sie
schon erwartet.
„Du bist wieder mal unpünktlich“,
sagt die Oberhexe streng.

„Aber die Hexenprüfung
hast du bestanden.
Wir haben
alles gesehen.
Das hast du
toll gemacht.“

Flora bekommt einen
nagelneuen Hexenbesen.
Dann feiert sie
mit den anderen
bis tief in die Nacht
ein wildes Hexenfest.

Das Hexenbad

„Es ist mal wieder so weit“,
sagt Max, der Rabe.
„Hm“, brummt Flora.
Sie liest gerade
die Hexenzeitung
und hört gar nicht zu.

„Es ist mal wieder so weit“,
sagt Max etwas lauter.
„Wovon redest du?“,
fragt Flora.
Max erklärt, dass es Zeit
für die Badewanne ist.

„Oh, nein!“, schreit Flora.
„Oh, doch!“, sagt Max.

Flora mag nicht baden.
Sie findet sich hexensauber.

Die Zehen sind schön schwarz.
Die Fingernägel haben
einen tollen, grünen Hexenrand.
Die Knie sind so grau,
wie sie sein sollen.
Und der Schmutz
in den Ohren
knistert so schön,
besonders
beim Einschlafen.

Sie mault:
„Ich habe vor zehn Jahren
erst gebadet."
„Vor genau zwanzig Jahren
und drei Monaten", sagt Max.

Flora sucht neue Ausreden.
In der Badewanne
wohnt Familie Goldfisch.

Max hat sie schon
in den Teich gebracht.

Flora hat
keinen Hexenschaum mehr.
Max weiß, wo das Rezept ist.

Max hilft rühren,
bis alles schön schäumt.
Er dreht den Wasserhahn auf.

Flora zieht sich aus.
„Aber ohne Haare waschen“,
knurrt sie.

Sie hält den dicken Zeh
ins Wasser.
„Warum badest du
eigentlich nicht, Max?“

„Ich bin doch keine Ente!“,
kräht Max empört.
„Ich etwa?“,
fragt Flora.

Dann liegt sie endlich
in der Wanne.
Das Wasser blubbert.
Max ist ganz erschöpft.

„Herrlich!“, seufzt Flora.
„Ich könnte bis Ostern
drin bleiben.“

„Immer dasselbe!“,
krächzt Max.

Der Geburtstag

Flora sitzt am Küchentisch.
Sie übt hexen.
Sie will alte Hüte
in Hexentorte
verwandeln.

Das ist schwierig.
Zuerst werden
aus den Hüten
harte Semmeln
und dann Spinat mit Spiegelei. Brrr!

Max sitzt
auf der Gardinenstange
und krächzt aus vollem Hals.

„Kannst du nicht leiser singen?“,
fragt Flora.
Max krächzt weiter.

Flora verhext die Hüte
in welke Salatköpfe.
„Du nervst!“,
knurrt sie.
Max krächzt weiter.

„Jetzt halt endlich
mal den Schnabel,
du Schreihals!“,
schreit Flora.
„Hast du etwa
Schreihals gesagt?“,
fragt Max wütend.

„Genau“, brüllt Flora.
„Schrecklicher Schreihals!“

„Du verstehst
überhaupt nichts
von Musik!“,
krächzt Max.

Beleidigt flattert er
auf und davon.

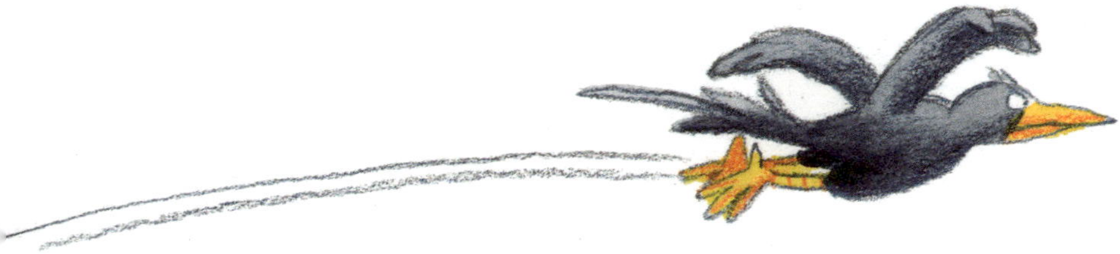

Jetzt ist es ruhig
in der Küche.
Flora will Hexentorte hexen.
Aber sie denkt an Max.
Aus den Hüten
werden Kürbisse.

Flora seufzt.
Wo ist Max bloß hingeflogen?

Am Abend ist Max
immer noch nicht zurück.
Und die Hüte sind
immer noch Hüte.

„Morgen ist mein Geburtstag“,
denkt Flora traurig.
„Aber ohne Max
und ohne Torte
bleibe ich lieber im Bett.“

Auch am Morgen ist Max
nirgends zu sehen.
Flora zieht sich die Decke
über den Kopf.

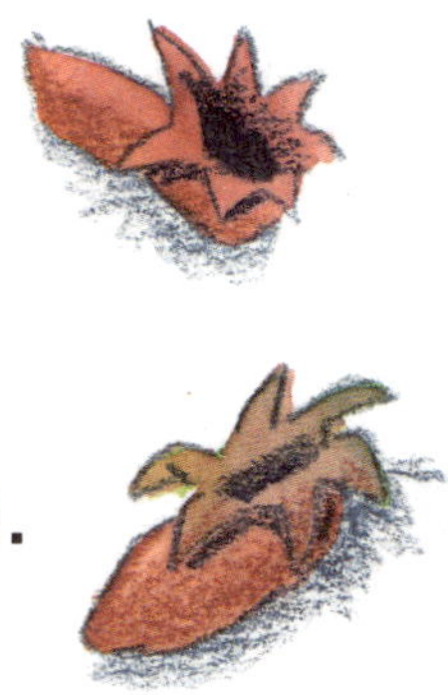

Da hört sie Stimmen im Garten.
Sie schlurft zur Tür.

Draußen stehen
die anderen Hexen.
Sie tragen eine große Hexentorte.

„Hast du nicht heute Geburtstag?“,
fragt die Moorhexe.

„Stimmt“, sagt Flora.
„Aber habt ihr Max gesehen?
Seit gestern ist er verschwunden!“

Doch niemand hat
den Raben gesehen.
Und ohne Max schmeckt
die beste Torte nicht.

Auf einmal krächzt es
oben im Baum.
Da sitzt Max
mit einem ganzen Raben-Orchester.

„Zum Geburtstag viel Glück“,
singt er. Und:
„Ich küsse Ihre Hand, Madame.“

„Schaurig-schön!“,
grummelt die Wurzelhexe.
Da singt Max als Zugabe:
„Ein Freund, ein guter Freund ...“

„Oh, Max!“, jubelt Flora.
„Ich sage auch nie mehr
Schreihals zu dir.“
Max grinst.